News Breaks

News Breaks

Compiled by Charles Keller
Illustrated by Michael Cooper

Prentice-Hall, Inc.

Englewood Cliffs, New Jersey

Printed in the United States of America

Prentice-Hall International, Inc., London
Prentice-Hall of Australia, Pty. Ltd., North Sydney
Prentice-Hall of Canada, Ltd., Toronto
Prentice-Hall of India Private Ltd., New Delhi
Prentice-Hall of Japan, Inc., Tokyo
Prentice-Hall of Southeast Asia Pte. Ltd., Singapore
Whitehall Books Limited, Wellington, New Zealand

10 9 8 7 6 5 4 3 2 1

Library of Congress Cataloging in Publication Data
Keller, Charles.
  News breaks.

  SUMMARY: Illustrated parodies of television news
broadcasts.
  1. American wit and humor.   2.   Wit and humor,
Juvenile.   [1.   Television broadcasting of news—
Anecdotes, facetiae, satire, etc.   2.   Wit and humor]
I.   Cooper, Michael, 1943-   II.   Title.
PN6163.K44   818'.5402   80-19573
ISBN 0-13-620583-6

For Nicole and Leigh

Other Books by Charles Keller

Canada sold the United States a large herd of bison and America received a buffalo bill.

Two freighters, one carrying red paint and the other carrying purple paint, collided yesterday. It is believed both crews are marooned.

A ship carrying a shipment of Yo-Yos across the ocean sprang a leak and sank 50 times.

Legislation for the preservation of waterfowl was not discussed in Congress today because everyone tried to duck the issue.

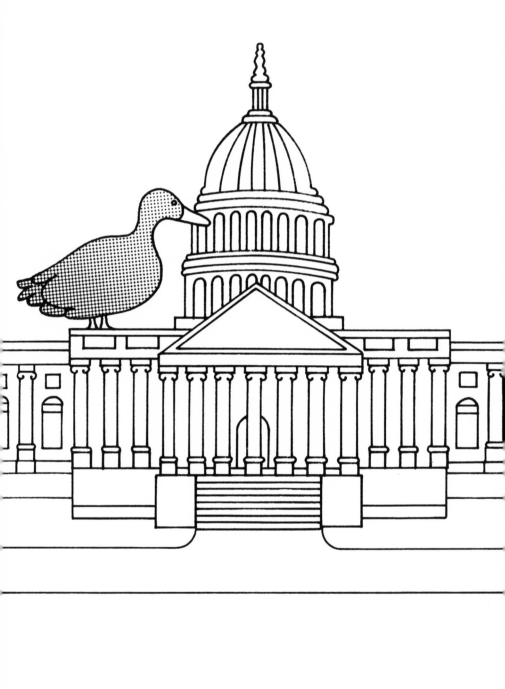

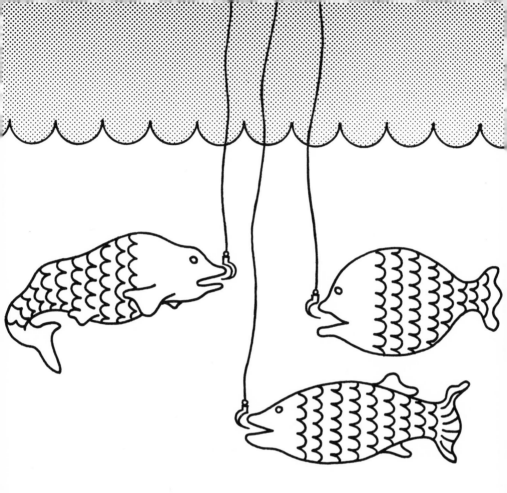

The cost of fish continues to rise and, as a result, fishhooks have really caught on.

A large shipment of hot dogs arrived from France because they owed us one million francs.

The post office announced it would begin shipping large fruit by boat. It is the first water-mailin'.

The two fruit companies merged. They say they make a perfect pair.

The price of duck feathers has increased and now even down is up.

The rodeo was a great success and one cowboy said he made a few bucks out of it.

Straw hats are out of style now, although they did have their hay day.

A new type of credit card was issued and people got a charge out of it.

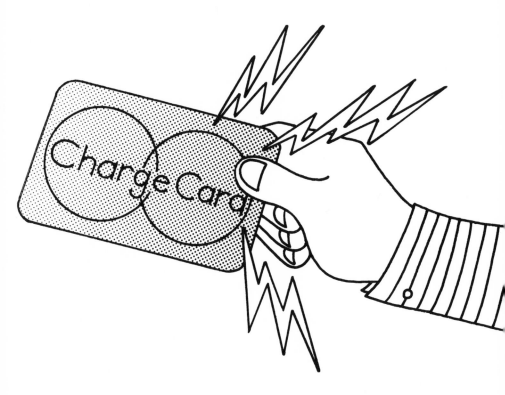

A new firecracker factory was opened and the owner says he is doing a booming business.

An orchestra leader hired a new assistant. He is the first band aid.

The price of sugar doubled and people began to raise cane.

The makers of boomerangs say that business is bad and they are trying for a comeback.

The users of new calculators have begun to multiply.

A new jigsaw puzzle came out recently and now the whole country is going to pieces.

Many people tagged along today as new license plates were distributed.

A new diet drive-in restaurant was opened for people who want to curb their appetites.

A new burlesque theater just opened, and one of the girls says she learned to imitate a stripper by doing a take-off.

A mini-sized tape recorder is being sold to people who like small-talk.

A new eye hospital opened and it was a site for sore eyes.

High heels are going out of style and women are in for a big letdown.

A new indoor tennis court was built and the builder made a good net profit.

A new escalator was installed at the shopping mall and everyone said it was a step in the right direction.

New metal dog leashes are being sold in chain stores.

Card playing was banned by the navy and the ships lost their decks.

The Railroad announced changes in their operation and now conductors will have to read a new training manual.

The price of sugar went down and the dealers took their lumps.

A golf course will stay open all night for people who like swinging nightclubs.

A penny sale was held at the super market and it made a lot of cents.

The pretzel baker closed his store because he got tired of making crooked dough.

A sardine factory closed and canned all its employees.

Business is slow everywhere and today a submarine sandwich restaurant went under.

A weight-reducing salon was closed because it was a losing proposition.

A tattoo parlor was closed because the artist had designs on his clients.

A massage parlor was closed for rubbing its customers the wrong way.

Miners called a strike saying that wearing the new illuminated helmets makes them feel lightheaded.

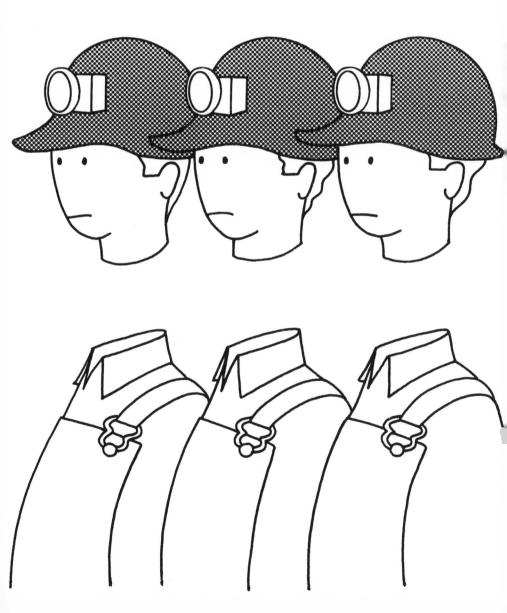

Artists' models went on strike saying they were barely making a living.

Longshoremen called a strike today and walked off the docks.

A bakers' strike was called because they wanted more dough.

Because of a strike at the cemetery gravedigging will be done by a skeleton crew.

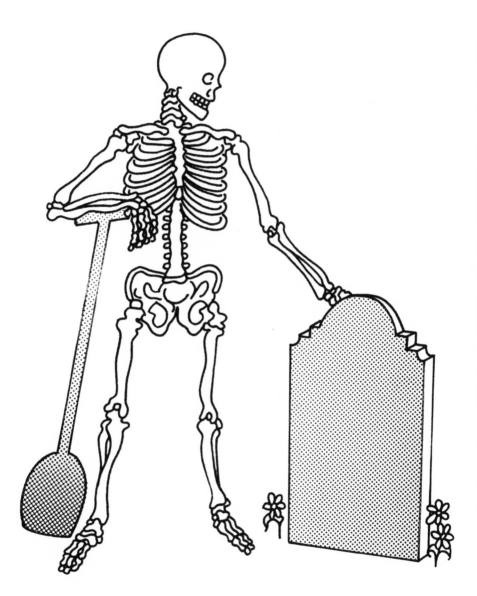

An employee in an automobile factory was fired for taking a break.

A man was fired because he put a watch in his mouth and gummed up the works.

The post office said it would begin firing over-age mailmen who have lost their zip.

An employee fell into a huge vat of gum and his boss really chewed him out.

An archaeologist complained that because of
bad publicity his career was in ruins.

A topless dancer was fired because she was unsuited for her work.

Eight sanitation workers were fired for not keeping their minds in the gutter.

The electricians' union held a meeting to discuss current events.

The janitors' union called for sweeping reforms.

The head of the airline pilots' union denied that they look down on people who don't fly.

The president of the tailors' union called a press conference today.

A new lumberjack union was formed by a splinter group.

A new headache pill was sold but people found it hard to swallow.

After twenty years of trial and error a new flypaper was discovered by a man who really stuck to his work.

A new non-slip-off watch band was introduced for people who can't afford to lose time.

A brand new hair coloring kit was introduced and it really got to the root of the problem.

A new branding iron was invented and the cattle were really impressed.

There's a new kind of rug being sold and the inventor says he is making a nice pile.

A mini-watch is being manufactured by a small-time operator.

Because of the introduction of a new type of calendar the days of the old ones are numbered.

A new type of women's stockings are being sold and there's a run on them.

The inventor of a new malted milk machine sold his patent and feels he got a good shake.

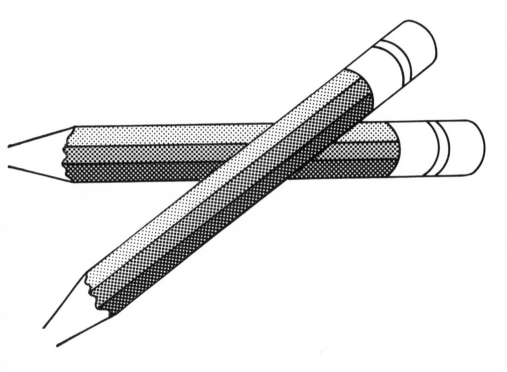

A new type of pencil was developed but people thought it was pointless.

Newsmen got a big scoop today as a new ice cream flavor was introduced.

A new kind of peanut was sold and the distributors say they will shell fast.

A new book on watchmaking was written and everyone thought it was about time.

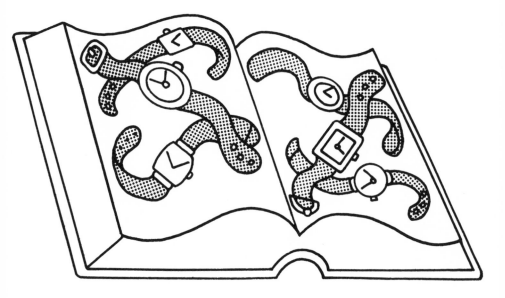

The inventor of a new packaging machine says he made a bundle.

A brand new thermometer is being manufactured by a man with many degrees.

A new kind of soda is being bottled. The inventor's son explained, "That's my pop."

A newly patented sandpaper was discovered by a man who really had it rough.

A new kind of walnut is being sold but people thought it wasn't what it was cracked up to be.

The next space satellite will contain cattle. It will be the herd shot around the world.

The first horse shelter was opened to provide animals with a stable environment.

A cookie factory burned down and everyone had free fire crackers.

There was a big fire at the shoe factory and over two thousand soles were lost.

No one was hurt at the disco fire because they hustled out of the place.

A broom factory burned but it was just a brush fire.

A Venetian blind company was raided by police who said it was being run by shady characters.

A man tried to make a pass at a librarian and the police threw the book at him.

A midget fortune-teller escaped from jail and the small medium is still at large.

Two hundred hares escaped from a rabbit farm; police are combing the area.

A man was robbed in Moscow and left without a
red cent.

A suspender factory was held up today.

People crashed a houseboat party by just barging in.

There's a nudist convention in town but it's receiving little coverage.

A munitions manufacturers' convention was held and it was a real blast.

The price of pigs went up and farmers went hog-wild.

Cranberry farmers announced a crop failure and said there would be no cranberry source.

Boll weevils are attacking the potato crops and farmers are told to keep their eyes peeled.

A dairy farmer says it's easy to milk a cow. Any jerk can do it.

A fortune teller sustained injuries when she told the Lone Ranger's fortune and he crossed her palm with Silver.

A sculptor celebrated his birthday and everyone
chipped in for a gift.

An ancient piece of stone was discovered with a multiplication problem carved on it. It was the first concrete example.

Cigarette lighters were given as prizes to tennis players who won a match.

A Scrabble contest was held and people sat down for a spell.

An art contest was held and the winners were chosen by a drawing.

A tree climbing contest was held for those who wanted to limber up.

A dinner was held for sculptors and marble cake was served for dessert.

Doctors report that people who go horseback riding feel better off.

A woman who was hard of hearing was treated with a new kind of ear drops and the next day she heard from her sister who was overseas.

A snake gave birth to a bouncing baby boa.

Siamese twins underwent surgery in Prague and emerged as separate Czechs.

A young boy was hospitalized when he swallowed two dimes, three nickels and seven pennies. Doctors have been treating him for 8 days but there is no change.

Doctors are treating a glass blower who got a pane in his stomach.

Plastic surgeons report that big noses usually run in some families.

A new medical report says that people who go to the doctor regularly don't live to regret it.

Doctors report that twenty million people are overweight. These are, of course, round figures.

A man was taken to the hospital when he put his head into a washing machine and got a sock in the face.

A guru refused to let his dentist use Novocaine because he wanted to transcend dental medication.

A baby doctor reports that if your child won't go to sleep just put him on the edge of the bed and he will soon drop off.

A doctor made the patient who swallowed a quarter cough up twenty dollars.

A new flea circus was started from scratch.

The human cannonball quit the circus and they are having trouble finding another man of his caliber.

The husband of the bearded lady says his wife ran away and gave him the brush-off.

The rubber man at the circus got bounced.

An accountant at the circus was fired for juggling the books.

A new magic act opened and it was so bad it made the audience disappear.

The magician was walking down the street and turned into a restaurant.

The Department of Motor Vehicles says that if your teenage son wants to learn to drive don't stand in his way.

An African explorer says that on his latest expedition several leopards were spotted.

An auto muffler shop owner says it's exhausting work.

Scientists report that if you want to be sure your children will go places buy them a chemistry set.

All young people do not make love in parked cars—the woods are full of them.

The Department of Education says that some guys who are poor in history are great on dates.

In the worm race two silkworms ended up in a tie.

At the greyhound races the biggest bet was won by a man with a hot dog.

A retired baseball player said he always had a ball.

A dozen swimmers began the big race. It started at the stroke of twelve.

The new heavyweight champ is making money hand over fist.

Baseball players refused to join a union because they didn't want to be called out on strikes.

During a five day bicycle race, the racers took a week end off.

In horse racing today in the third race "Poison Ivy" was scratched.

Charles Keller, the author of nineteen collections of children's humor for Prentice-Hall, was born in New York City. He is a graduate of St. Peter's College and now lives on top of the Palisades in Union City, New Jersey.

Michael Cooper, graphic designer for television, illustrator for magazines, and creator of books for children, lives in New York City.